With special thanks to Martin Handford for the Wally spread,
Anthony Horowitz for *Secret Weapon*, and Sam Stern for his pizza recipe.

With contributions from: Andreas Samuelsson, Cristina Guitian, Matthew Hodson,
Jim Medway, Nigel Coan, and Andrew Wightman.

Cover © 2010 Walker Books Ltd

First published 2008 by Walker Books Ltd, 87 Vauxhall Walk, London SE11 5HJ
and Short Books Ltd, 3A Exmouth House, Pine Street, London EC1R OJH

J271.725 €6.00

This edition published 2010

2 4 6 8 10 9 7 5 3 1

Copyright © 2008, 2010 WAWWD Community Interest Company 05241856
Spread from *Where's Wally? The Wonder Book* © 1997 Martin Handford

Secret Weapon © 2003 Anthony Horowitz.
Trademark 2008 Stormbreaker Productions Ltd.
Alex Rider ™

Pizza recipe from *Real Food, Real Fast.*
© 2006 Susan and Sam Stern

Printed in China

Mixed Sources
Product group from well-managed
forests and other controlled sources
www.fsc.org Cert no. SCS-COC-000927
© 1996 Forest Stewardship Council
FSC

British Library Cataloguing in Publication Data: a catalogue record for
this book is available from the British Library

ISBN 978-1-4063-2715-1

www.walker.co.uk

www.shortbooks.co.uk

31 Ways to Change the World

by 4,386 children,

we are what we do© and YOU!

Produced by **Nick Stanhope**
Art direction and design by **New Future Graphic**
Written by **Tanis Taylor**...
& 4,386 children (more or less)

WALKER
BOOKS

✳ SHORT BOOKS

CHANGING THE WORLD

That seems a pretty massive task. Not the sort of thing you squeeze in before breakfast or tick off while you're tying your shoelaces. "Yup, done. Next job!" Surely not?

But it turns out that there's loads of stuff that takes not very long at all that can really change things.

Big things.

Like global warming, bullying, animal rights and why people don't smile more. **Curious?**

You do things, every day. Small things that don't even take five minutes. Let's call them **"actions"**. You take showers. You eat chicken nuggets. You buy stuff. You fart. J271.725 £6.00

Over our lifetime these actions add up. You will spend **6,000 hours in the shower**. You will eat **1,201 chickens** (or nutloaves if you're a veggie). You will buy **678,740 things**. (Wow!) And you will fart **421,575 times**. (Now that's not to be sniffed at.)

You have a HUGE impact on the world around you. Every day, your actions and your choices influence things – from your mates and your mum, to chicken farmers and factory workers in Africa.

So in those few minutes when you're brushing your teeth or choosing a sarnie from the supermarket, you're having an effect that could last, well, maybe forever...

At **We Are What We Do** we believe that by making small changes to your everyday actions, you can make a BIG difference.

And that when lots and lots of us make small changes to our everyday actions – together – we can

CHANGE THE WORLD.

Amazing!

The science bit:

small actions x lots of people
= BIG CHANGE

We've got 131 of these small actions (and the list keeps growing...). Actions 1–100 are in our other books and you can find them on our website www.wearewhatwedo.org.

And the thirty-one in this book? Where are they from? Well, we asked the most imaginative people we knew for some ideas. We asked you. We got loads of children (well 4,386) to give us their suggestions and hand-picked the best gems. Thirty-one amazing, everyday actions. By children. For children.

Actions that everyone can do. In not very long. To change the world.

They are small.
They are strange.
But do them with others
And things will change.

Go on. Get stuck in. Try Erica's Action 115 and teach your granny to text. Why? Because when you do it, you get to spend time with someone from a different generation. Because if we all did it there would be millions of grandparents who could stay in touch better. Because you know stuff. And Grans know stuff. And because we should all swap stuff. Unplug Sammah's Action 122. Pump up Omar's Action 129. Give away Emma's Action 120. And when you're done, pester everyone into doing YOUR amazing Action 131.

Find five minutes between picking your nose and cleaning out your hamster and give one a go.

You can change anything and everything that matters to you – from how your house recycles and how green your teacher is, to fat dads and gloomy mates.

Start here ... continue online and out there and who knows where it will end. Happy world changing!

Make someone smile

There are some people who hardly ever smile. You could call them grumpy-lumps. We call them challenges.

Make someone smile – for no reason in particular.

Fact: It takes half as many muscles to smile as it does to frown.

Thank you for a lovely tea.

8

How do you catch a squirrel?

Climb a tree and act like a nut!

You see 300 people every day. If one million kids smile at 300 people each, every person in Britain will get smiled at. Five times.

I saw this and I thought of you x

YO, WHAT'S UP?

Walk your dad

Like dogs, grown-ups get cranky when they stay indoors all 🕐 DAY LONG. Unlike dogs - who walk an average of 676 miles a year - dads walk just 197. KEEP them off the furniture: take a grown-up for A WALK.

SNIFF SNIFF

uhhhhh...

Grow something & eat it

Take a tiny seed and turn it into something amazing. Go on. I dare you.

Why not try basil? It's easy to grow and tastes great - especially on a pizza!

All you need are some seeds, a sunny windowsill and a pot of nice soil with a hole in the bottom.

Make sure you keep your seedlings watered but not too wet.

BLIMEY! It's growing! HOORAY!!

HOME GROWN FOOD
It's easy! It's free!
It's amazing!!
No wasteful packaging!
No supermarket queues!
WARNING:
May contain bugs.

As soon as there are plenty
of leaves, pinch them off
and scatter them on top
of Action 110.

Stand up for something

If a friend was being bullied you could wait for someone else to do something.

If your school wasn't recycling you could wait for your Head to do something.

If the planet was heating up you could wait for the government to do something.

Personally, we hate waiting.

Speak up.

Change your world.

Starting from now.

Photography: Stephen Morgan

In twenty years from now,
When all the power's gone,
We'll remember all those rooms
With their standby lights left on.
We'll say, "I wish we'd turned
Them off, those pretty little lights!
Who knew they'd suck our planet dry
While we slept through the night?"

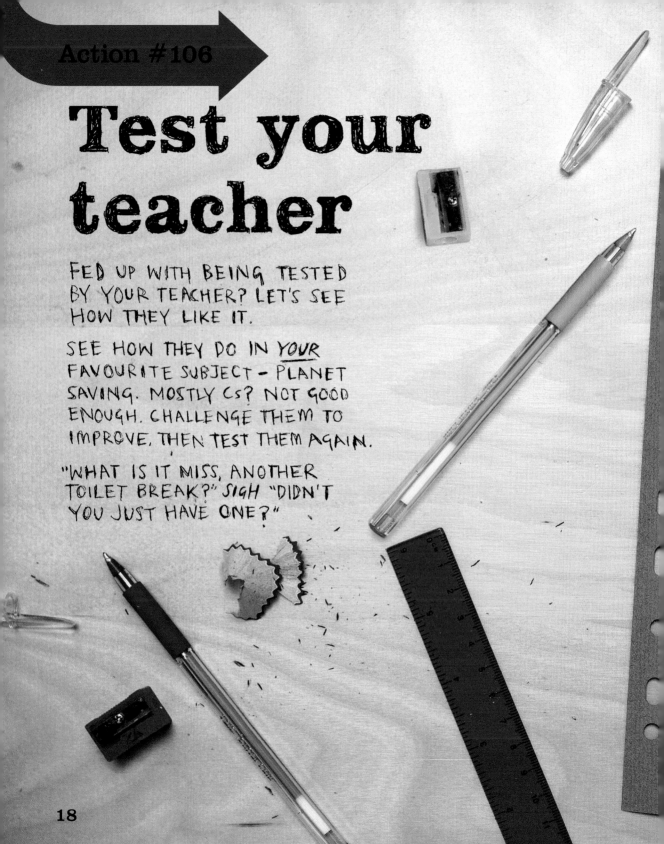

Test your teacher

FED UP WITH BEING TESTED BY YOUR TEACHER? LET'S SEE HOW THEY LIKE IT.

SEE HOW THEY DO IN _YOUR_ FAVOURITE SUBJECT – PLANET SAVING. MOSTLY Cs? NOT GOOD ENOUGH. CHALLENGE THEM TO IMPROVE, THEN TEST THEM AGAIN.

"WHAT IS IT MISS, ANOTHER TOILET BREAK?" SIGH "DIDN'T YOU JUST HAVE ONE?"

THE BIG GREEN TEST FOR TEACHERS

1 At home

a. How many of your lightbulbs are low-energy?
  A. All
  B. Some
  C. None

b. What temperature do you normally wash your clothes on?
  A. 30°
  B. 40°
  C. 50°+

c. Are you a composter?.
  A. Yes
  B. No
  C. A what?!

d. How often do you leave things on stand-by?
  A. Never
  B. Sometimes
  C. Always

e. Do you charge your mobile phone overnight?
  A. Never
  B. Sometimes
  C. Always

f. Do you turn the tap off when you brush your teeth?
  A. Always
  B. When I remember!
  C. Never

2 Travelling about

a. How do you travel to school?
  A. Walk, cycle, on public transport
  B. In a full car of people
  C. In a car on my own

b. Do you check that your tyres are pumped up to the right pressure levels? (Helps your car use less fuel!)
  A. Regularly
  B. Occasionally
  C. Never

c. How do you travel if your journey's less than a mile?
  A. Walk or cycle
  B. Public transport
  C. Car

d. How many flights do you take every year?
  A. None
  B. One or two
  C. More than three

3 At school

a. Do you use both sides of the paper when you photocopy?
  A. Always
  B. Sometimes
  C. Never

b. Do you have recycling bins in the staff room?
  A. Yes, for everything!
  B. Yes, for paper
  C. No, none

c. How much water do you boil to make a cup of tea?
  A. Just as much as I need
  B. A bit more than I need
  C. A full kettle almost always

d. Do you print on recycled paper?
  A. Always
  B. Sometimes
  C. Never

4 How did you score?

Mostly As: Bright Green. Well done. Hats off. You are qualified to teach me in the ways of the world as you are a big, green, shining beacon. Teacher, I salute you.

Mostly Bs: Light Green. You might know your stuff in the classroom, but you won't win any prizes for planet-saving. Strong start, but you must try harder.

Mostly Cs: Limp Green. Oh dear, we have a problem. If this doesn't improve, not only will the planet go "pop", but you will have to see me after class.

Look closer

Sometimes it pays to take your time. To look closer, to find the things no one else does. It makes you good at Where's Wally? It makes you good at life.

Ten of our actions have wandered into Wally's world. Can you find them? (And him).

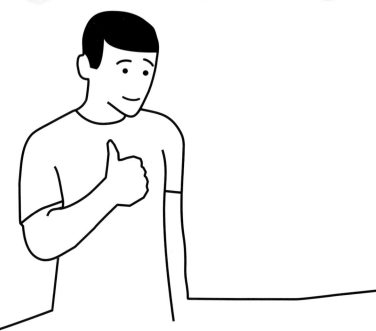

Be friendly in sign language

"All right?"

A bit of sign language always comes in handy. Use it in quiet places (libraries). Use it in loud places (football matches). Use it to make 9 million new friends.*

Illustration: New Future Graphic

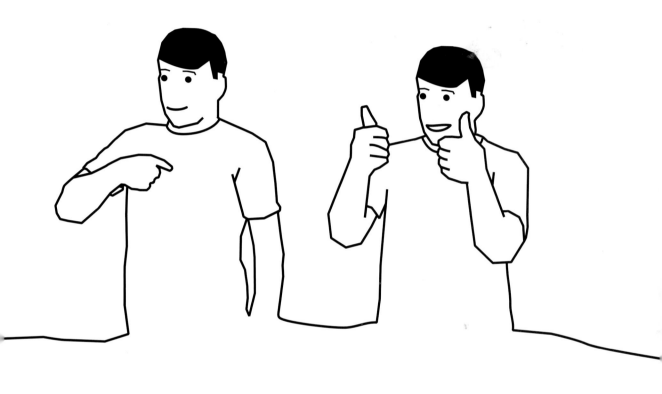

"I'm fantastic!"

* There are estimated to be about 9 million deaf and hard of hearing people in the UK. And more than 34,000 deaf children and young people.

Layer up

What is our greatest weapon against global warming?

Science? Biofuel? Solar power?

Nu-huh. It's the sweater. The next time it gets chilly, put a sweater on.

Not the heating.

In 1970 the average temperature of a British house was 12°C. Today it is 19°C.

Is your central heating making you fat? When our houses are cooler our bodies burn calories and keep us nice and toasty.

The first radiator was invented in 1855. Before that people wore bigger jumpers. And hugged more.

Cook a meal from scratch

Your mission, should you choose to accept it, is dinner for two. Cook it from scratch. Using only raw ingredients.

Your secret weapon? Sam Stern, teenage chef. Good luck.

(And call us when it's ready)

MARGHERITA PIZZA - SERVES 2

PIZZA BASE:

450 g/1lb STRONG WHITE
BREAD FLOUR
1 TSP SALT
1 TSP CASTER SUGAR
2 x 7G SACHET FAST ACTION
DRIED YEAST
300 ML/½ PINT WARM WATER
2 TSPS GOOD OLIVE OIL

PIZZA TOPPING:

2 x 150g BALL MOZZARELLA
1 x 400g CAN
CHOPPED TOMATOES
1 CLOVE GARLIC,
CRUSHED
FEW BLACK OLIVES
SALT AND BLACK PEPPER
OLIVE OIL

A FEW LEAVES OF
ACTION 103

SAM'S MARGHERITA PIZZA

1. SIFT FLOUR AND SALT INTO A BOWL. ADD SUGAR AND YEAST.

2. POUR IN WATER AND OLIVE OIL. WORK DOUGH INTO A SOFT BALL. ADD A DROP MORE WATER IF NEEDED.

3. SLAP DOUGH ONTO A LIGHTLY FLOURED BOARD. PUNCH, PULL, THUMP AND KNEAD FOR 10 MIN UNTIL SOFT AND ELASTIC.

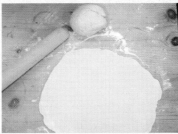

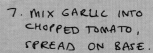

4. LEAVE COVERED IN A WARM PLACE FOR 1 HOUR, OR UNTIL DOUBLED IN SIZE.

5. LIGHTLY OIL TWO BAKING TRAYS. DIVIDE DOUGH INTO TWO EQUAL BALLS AND ROLL OUT FLAT. LEAVE COVERED ON BAKING TRAYS TO RISE AGAIN FOR 15 MIN.

6. PREHEAT OVEN TO 230°C/400°F/GAS 6

7. MIX GARLIC INTO CHOPPED TOMATO, SPREAD ON BASE.

8. CHUCK ON SLICED MOZZARELLA, OLIVES, SEASONING. DRIZZLE WITH A LITTLE OLIVE OIL.

9. BAKE 15-20 MIN. SERVE WITH A SCATTERING OF ACTION 103.

Love your stuff

New stuff comes in nice packaging.

It smells good and has fancy tags.

Old stuff doesn't. It's flat from being at the bottom of your bed. Or smelly from being your favourite football shirt. It's full of holes.

And you've earned every one of them.

Love your stuff. To bits.

I love snakey cos he scares my brother

I have had he for a long tim

I love taking pictures of things that I love

I've had it since I was a baby

This turtle remind me of my grand

He's got good clothes

It reminds me of being in Portugal

football is my best subject

I love Tom because I got him when I was a baby

I will always love her.

He can be moody but I don't care.

She is always happy

Because we have good hugs

This is my first trophy.

Go to more parties

Merry Bean-Throwing Day!

Happy Diwali!

Groundhog Greetings!

The great thing about having friends from other cultures is that you get to go to all their parties. We've taken the liberty of putting a few dates in your diary.

JANUARY

Burns' night
A Scottish celebration of the life of poet Robert Burns on 25th January (Robert Burns wrote "Auld Lang Syne". (All together now...)

The Lantern Festival
On the fifteenth day of the first month the streets are lit with glowing, colourful lanterns to mark the end of the Chinese New Year and welcome new beginnings. Children stroll the streets holding home-made lanterns.

FEBRUARY

Groundhog Day
If the groundhog (also known as a woodchuck or ground squirrel) emerges from his burrow on 2nd February and doesn't see his shadow, it means winter will soon end. If he does see his shadow, it's back into his hole, and winter for six more weeks... Boo.

Carnival
Four days before Ash Wednesday every year, the streets of Rio de Janeiro in Brazil come alive with parties, festivals and samba bands. The crowds wear colourful outfits covered with feathers and sequins, and children practise for months to perform in dancing bands.

Illustration: Andreas Samuelsson

Rissun

This Shinto celebration on 3rd February marks the end of winter and the chasing away of evil spirits. People throw handfuls of beans into any dark corners while shouting, "Fortune in, Devils out!"

MARCH

St David's Day

Saint David is the patron saint of Wales and 1st March is his feast day. People celebrate Welsh culture and history and wear daffodils or leeks in their lapels.

Doll's Festival

A day for girls! In Japan young girls display dolls in traditional dress on a platform in their house. Throughout the festival, families visit shrines to pray for girls' health and happiness.

Holi

This Hindu festival from India is nicknamed the "Festival of Colours" because during the day people spill out onto the streets and throw huge amounts of coloured powder and water at each other!

APRIL

Children's Day

This day is celebrated throughout Turkey to remind people that children are the future. Turkish children dress in national dress and perform in plays and musicals, and the seats in parliament are held by children for one day only.

Vaisakhi

One of the most important holidays in the Sikh calendar, this is a time to remember the birth of Sikhism in 1699. People clean and decorate their local Gudwaras (the Sikh place of worship) with flowers, and bathe themselves to purify body and soul before celebrating with parades, dancing and singing. Children start the practice of charity on this day and continue it throughout the year.

Pesach

Pesach or "Passover" is an eight-day feast celebrating the end of slavery for the Jewish people when they fled Egypt, and their arrival in Israel. People eat "matzo", a flatbread, to remind them that when they left Egypt it was in such a rush that their bread didn't have time to rise.

MAY

Cheese Rolling

Since the nineteenth-century, competitors in Gloucestershire have taken part in this event: a round of Double Gloucester cheese is rolled from the top of a steep hill and they all try to catch it. Since the cheese can reach speeds of 70mph, this is quite a challenge!

Baby-Jumping Festival

In the village of Castrillo de Murcia in Spain, grown men dressed as devils leap over a row of helpless babies! As they jump they take all the evil with them and cleanse the children.

Vesak

The most important event of the Buddhist calendar, Vesak, or Buddha's Day, celebrates the Buddha's birth, death and enlightenment. Homes are cleaned and decorated. Flowers, candles and joss-sticks are left at the feet of statues. People eat vegetarian food, and caged animals, insects and birds are ceremonially freed.

JUNE

Dragon Boat Festival

When a famous Chinese poet called Qu Yuan was drowned, the townsfolk took to their boats, beating drums and throwing dumplings into the water to scare away fish and stop creatures from eating his body. Today, teams of twenty-two paddlers take to the water in long dragon boats and race to the sound of drums.

Alien Festival

Legend has it that a UFO crashed in Roswell, New Mexico, USA, in 1947 and each year people dressed as aliens go there to parade and party. The truth is out there … somewhere.

Tomato Fight

The biggest food fight in the world, this Spanish festival involves 110,000 kilos of tomatoes being thrown at anyone you can manage to hit. "Hey slowcoach, ketchup!"

Raksha Bandhan

A Hindu festival for brothers and sisters marked by the tying of a holy thread, by the sister, onto the wrist of her brother. In return the brother promises to look after her and they feed each other sweets. (No brother, no worries! Any male can be "adopted" as a brother for the occasion.)

Summer Solstice

Solstice comes from the Latin for "sun stands still" and the Summer Solstice is when the sun is at its highest elevation of the year. The Celts celebrated with bonfires to add to the sun's energy and in the UK today, pagans and druids dance and light fires to greet the sunrise at Stonehenge's stone circle.

Grandmothers' Festival

A grand old celebration of grandmothers in Norway. This festival sees grannies riding motorbikes and race-horses, skydiving and scuba diving.

SEPTEMBER

AUGUST

JULY

World Pillow Fighting Championships

Competitors sit, facing each other, on the top of a slippery pole above a mud-pit. Using only a pillow they must unseat their opponent. Rounds last one minute. Feathers will fly.

Highland Games

What better way to celebrate Scotland than these games that came down from the Highlands. Cabers (long pine logs) are tossed and heavy stones thrown while bagpipes are played and kilts worn.

Ramadan

Ramadan is a month of fasting from sunrise to sunset. During Ramadan, Muslims pray and fast, celebrating the time when the verses of the Qur'an were revealed to the Prophet Muhammad. The Islamic holiday of Eid marks the end of Ramadan.

Ethiopian New Year's Day

The start of the New Year in Ethiopia on 11th September is a colourful affair, with priests walking around their churches with bright umbrellas and colourful holy books. Rastafarians believe Ethiopia is their spiritual homeland, so they celebrate this too.

Diwali

Diwali is the Festival of Light, celebrated by Sikhs, Hindus and Jains. In Britain, as in India, the festival is a time for spring-cleaning the home, for wearing new clothes and, most importantly, for decorating buildings with lights.

Monkey Buffet

In Thailand, locals gather together and lay on a magnificent buffet of fruit and vegetables for the monkeys that roam free. Around 600 of them turn up to take advantage of this free meal!

NOVEMBER

DECEMBER

OCTOBER

Day of the Dead

Mexican people pray to the souls of dead relatives on this day and ask them to return for one night. They decorate their homes with skulls, dress as skeletons and parade through the streets. Bread is even baked in the shape of a skull! This festival remembers dead relatives and celebrates their lives.

Christmas

An annual Christian holiday that celebrates the birth of Jesus. Children receive gifts and cards from Santa Claus and Christmas trees are dressed with baubles and decorations and topped with a star to represent the Star of Bethlehem from the Nativity story.

Halloween

Legend has it that, on 31st October, the boundary between the dead and the living gets blurred. So to confuse those dastardly spirits, dress as a ghoul yourself! Boo.

Santa Lucia

On 13th December, one of winter's longest, darkest nights, girls in Sweden dress up as Santa Lucia in a white dress and a crown of candles. The day is a big feast day and boys may dress as gingerbread men, while sweet Lucia buns are eaten in celebration.

Oktoberfest

A jolly German festival where the women wear a traditional outfit called a "dirndl" and men wear "lederhosen" or leather trousers. Meat is eaten, beer is drunk and there is much singing and good cheer.

33

Ask "Why?"

Years ago someone looked up into the night sky and asked: "Why can't we build something powerful enough to take man to the moon?" The rest, as thay say, is history.

WHY DO WE HAVE SCHOOL?

WHY IS THE SKY BLUE?

WHY DO WE WALK UPRIGHT?

WHY DO CHILDREN STILL DIE OF HUNGER WHEN THERE IS ENOUGH FOOD IN THE WORLD?

WHY DO SOME PEOPLE GROW TALLER THAN OTHERS?

WHY ISN'T EVERYONE THE SAME RELIGION?

WHY DO WE REMEMBER SOME THINGS AND NOT OTHERS? WHY DO CROCODILES EAT ROCKS?

WHY ARE LEAVES GREEN?

WHY ARE THERE LEAP YEARS?

WHY DO WE EXIST?

WHY DO WE NEED FOOD?

WHY IS A DAY TWENTY FOUR HOURS?

WHY DO WE WEAR CLOTHES?

WHAT QUESTION WOULD YOU ASK?

MARKS THE SPOT

Love where you live

Maps can be boring. But they don't have to be.

Why not make your own map? Fill it with places you've discovered and things you love around where you live. Fill it with the stuff other kids would actually want to know.

Put your neighbourhood on the map.

GOOD HILL TO RIDE DOWN REALLY FAST !!!

WHERE U LIVE!

Illustration Ned Selby

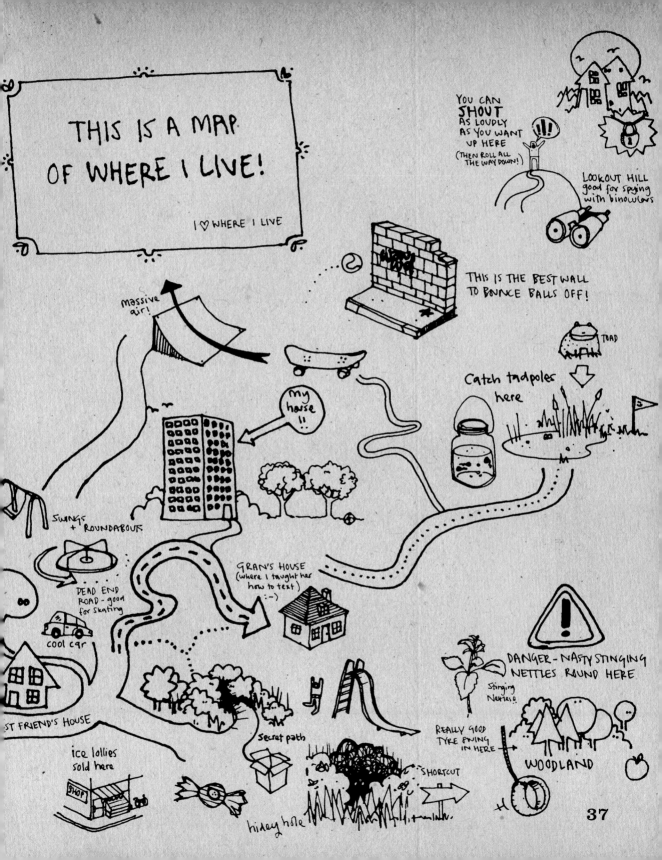

Teach Your Granny to Text

IMD = In my day...
NE14T? = Anyone for tea?
FDLSTX = fiddlesticks
RNGPNTT? = Bingo tonight?

CUL8R = See you later!

WHERERMY-oo-? = Where are my glasses?

YYY = you young things

UHTSMCKZNMLK? = Do you want some cookies and milk?

HBTU = Happy Birthday to you

HNTU* = Haven't you grown

IYKTDUSMLUYISOK = I've knitted you some lovely socks *

Find out about your food

Our food had a whole life before it reached our table.

What's your apple's life story?

I never had what you would call my own room. I grew up on an English "farm" with 30,000 other chickens. I can tell you, it's good preparation for being in a chicken sandwich, being squashed up with that lot. I hear there are other farms where chickens get more space. To perch, peck, cluck about. I dunno. Sounds egg-straordinary to me.

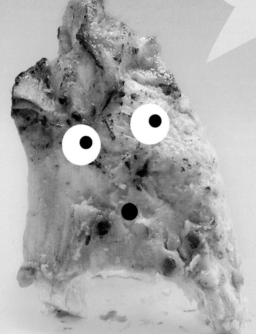

41

Read with a pal

It's just plain rude to keep a good Alex Rider story all to yourself...

SECRET WEAPON
© Anthony Horowitz

The man with the two missing teeth had thought a great deal about killing Alex Rider. He had imagined it. He had planned it. Today he was going to do it.

His name was Skoda. At least, that was what he had called himself when he had been a drug dealer in west London. He had sold his little packets of death in pubs, at street corners and outside schools until the day he had made just one mistake. He had chosen Brookland School and that was how he had met Alex.

Skoda thought about that as he sat outside the school, ten months later, watching and waiting. It still seemed impossible. He had been living on a canal boat. The 14-year-old schoolboy had used a crane to hook the boat out of the water and had dropped it – from a height – into the middle of a police conference. Skoda had been arrested immediately. Worse than that; he had become a laughing stock throughout the criminal world. Skoda doubted that Alex would recognize him now. He still had the missing teeth and pierced ears. But the incident with the canal boat had left terrible scars. They had patched him up in hospital but the stitch marks still showed. They began high on his forehead, ran the length of his nose, continued through his mouth and ended under his chin. The two halves of his face had been sewn back together by a doctor who had obviously never trained in cosmetic surgery. He looked hideous.

But Alex Rider would pay. Skoda had escaped from the prison hospital. He had made enquiries and he had finally discovered who he had to blame for his misfortunes. He knew he would be arrested again eventually. But that didn't matter.

Today it would be his turn to laugh.

Alex was coming out of drama when he ran into the new teacher … literally. He was in a crowd of half a dozen boys and they were all breaking one of the ten commandments of Brookland School: thou shalt not run in the corridors.

Somehow the others managed to get out of her way. Alex crashed into her.

Everyone had been talking about June Summers since she had arrived, just a few weeks ago. She was a supply teacher – physics and chemistry – and suddenly everyone wanted to do science. Miss Summers was young, still in her twenties, and almost absurdly attractive with blonde hair falling to her shoulders, amazing blue eyes and movie star lips. She dressed like a teacher with a grey, tailored jacket and serious shoes. But she walked like a model. The boys joked about her. And Alex had just run into her. It was the first time they'd met.

"Good morning," she said. "I'm Miss Summers."

"I'm sorry..." Alex bent down and picked up her papers for her.

She looked at him coolly. "You're Alex Rider," she said.

"Yes." He wondered how she knew.

"I've been looking at your reports from last term. You've got a lot of catching up to do."

"I was away … sick."

"You seem to get sick a lot," Miss Summers said.

Alex couldn't tell her the truth. He couldn't tell anyone. Even if he had been allowed to, nobody would have believed him.

He had no parents. He had been brought up by an uncle – Ian Rider – who had been a spy, working in an obscure department of MI6 … a secret within a secret. Then his uncle had died and somehow they had manipulated Alex into taking his place. There were times, they had said, when a child could achieve things that an adult could not. And if he missed school? If he came back each time, not just injured but with his whole life bent out of shape? It didn't matter. He was doing it for his country. Nobody must know.

Of course, Miss Summers was right. Despite his efforts to catch up, Alex was slipping behind in class. She had read his reports. His form teacher: "Alex is a bright and pleasant boy but he would be doing much better if he turned up more regularly at school…"

And humanities: "Alex needs to join in more and to be part of the class. He was absent again this term. But he wrote a first-class essay on Russian politics and the collapse of the fleet at Murmansk."

That had amused Alex. What he'd learned about Murmansk hadn't come out of a book. If it hadn't been for him, Murmansk – along with half of Russia – would no longer exist.

Miss Summers was still watching him with those deep, blue eyes. "Are you going on the trip this afternoon?" she asked.

"Yes, Miss."

"Are you interested in weapons?"

Alex thought briefly of all the guns and knives that, at different times, had been aimed at him. "Yes," he said.

"Well, enjoy it. But don't run in the corridor."

She took back her papers and then she was gone, brushing past him and disappearing into the staff room. Alex wondered what she did when she wasn't working as a supply teacher. A bell rang. Walking fast, he headed for the next class.

The exhibition at the British Museum was called Seven Hundred Years of War and had hundreds of weapons – from medieval bows to automatic machine guns – displayed in a dozen galleries. Two classes from Brookland had gone, with Miss Summers and Mr Bryce (who

taught history) in charge. It was the last visit of the day. The museum was about to close.

Later, Alex would be unsure quite how he had managed to lag behind. He had been looking at a case of replica guns. MI6 never let him have a gun. Maybe that was why he was interested. At the same time, he had become aware of a security guard showing the other visitors out of the gallery, before slowly walking over to him. The guard seemed to have been involved in a bad car accident. His face was divided by a line of stitches.

"Enjoying yourself?" the guard asked.

Alex shrugged.

"If you like weapons, you might be interested in this one."

The guard smiled and that was what saved Alex. The two missing teeth. Instantly, Alex knew he had seen the man before – and he was already moving, sliding backwards as the fake guard suddenly produced a vicious sword, taken from the kung fu gallery next door. It was a unicorn sword, also called lin jiao dao, 15th century, Chinese. It had three razor-sharp blades: one about a metre long and the others shorter, attached to the handle and shaped like lethal crescent moons. The guard had aimed for his head. As Alex leapt back, he actually felt the sword slice the air, less than a centimetre from his face.

The guard came at him a second time, stabbing forward now with the three blades. Alex only just managed to avoid them, hampered by his school uniform and backpack. He twisted back, lost his balance and fell. He heard the man laugh out loud as his shoulders crashed into the wooden floor and the breath was knocked out of him.

The guard walked forward, spinning the sword. That was when Alex remembered his name.

"Skoda!" he said.

"You remember me?"

"I never forget a face. But something seems to have happened to yours."

Alex tried to get up but Skoda pushed him back with the sole of his foot.

"You did this to me," he snarled and Alex saw that the two halves of his head no longer worked at the same time. It was as if two people were fighting for control of his mouth. "And now you're going to pay!" Skoda giggled. "This is going to be slow. This is going to hurt!"

He raised the sword. There was nothing Alex could do. For once, he was helpless, on his back – with no gadgets, no clever moves. Skoda took a breath. He was like a butcher examining a prime cut of meat. His tongue hung out. It was also

stitched in two halves. There was a soft thudding sound. Skoda pitched forward and lay still. There was a small, feathered dart sticking out of his neck. Alex looked past him and his head swam. Miss Summers was standing there, holding a tranquilliser gun.

"Are you hurt, Alex?" she asked.

Alex got unsteadily to his feet. "You…?" he began. He was staring at the gun.

"It's all right," Miss Summers said. "I'm with MI6." She touched the unconscious drug dealer with the tip of her shoe. "We knew Skoda had escaped. We were afraid he might come after you. I was sent in to keep an eye on you."

"You're a spy?"

"I think the words you're looking for are – thank you!"

It was true. She had just saved his life. Alex looked around him. Seven hundred years of war. He was part of it now and had been ever since his uncle had died. MI6 had made him their secret weapon. They had put him into a glass case of their own and they were the ones with the key.

"Thank you, Miss Summers," he said.

"Don't mention it, Alex," Miss Summers replied. "Now, you'd better go down and find the others while I deal with our friend." She smiled at him. "And try to remember not to run!"

Don't sing in the shower

The average shower lasts seven minutes and uses 35 litres of water.

Actually, two minutes is all it takes to soap up, wash down, scrub your armpits, do your rude bits and still have time for your hair. If everyone in your class took two minute showers for a year, with the water saved you could fill an entire swimming pool. And then some.

Take shorter showers. Save your singing for the rain.

(PS Shorter showers also mean longer lie-ins. Which is almost as good as saving the world.)

Illustration: Andrew Wightman

47

Play

OK, so we lied.
Not all of the actions are in
the book. This one's outside.
Waiting to happen.

You still here? Go play!

Photography: New Future Graphic

Give lots of compliments

Compliments get easier when you do them regularly. So make a 5-a-day habit of giving them away. They cost nothing. Thay make you feel good. Everyone accepts them. And a good one can last for weeks.

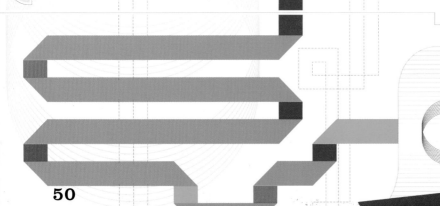

1

○ VOUCHER — *give one get one free!*

TO: Samantha · Monday

COMPLIMENT:

I like your hair

SIGNED Selan

2

○ VOUCHER — *give one get one free!*

TO: Noah · march 21

COMPLIMENT: You are good in goal

SIGNED Sam

3

○ VOUCHER — *give one get one free!*

TO: Cara thornton · monday

COMPLIMENT: I LIKE sitting Next to you

SIGNED Sophie B.

4

○ VOUCHER — *give one get one free!*

TO: Mohammed · June 1

COMPLIMENT:

You look happy

SIGNED Tahir

5

○ VOUCHER — *give one get one free!*

TO: cara · 21/3

COMPLIMENT: you make me laugh

SIGNED Eugenie

Stop junk mail

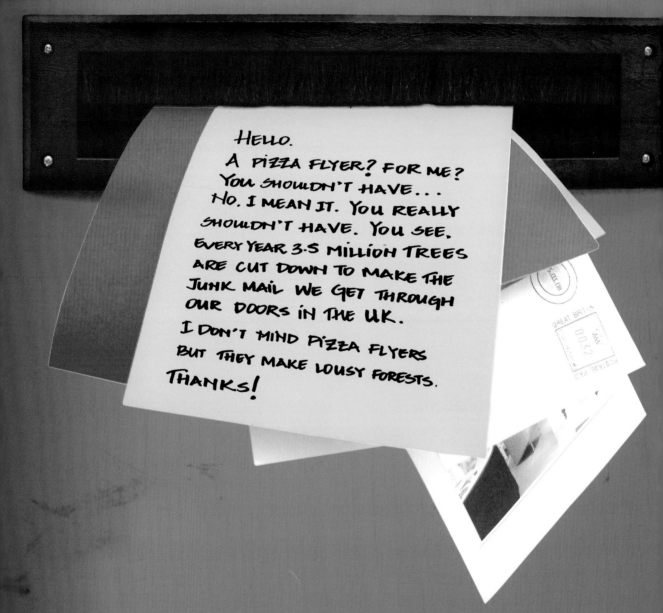

HELLO.
A PIZZA FLYER? FOR ME?
YOU SHOULDN'T HAVE...
NO. I MEAN IT. YOU REALLY
SHOULDN'T HAVE. YOU SEE.
EVERY YEAR 3.5 MILLION TREES
ARE CUT DOWN TO MAKE THE
JUNK MAIL WE GET THROUGH
OUR DOORS IN THE UK.
I DON'T MIND PIZZA FLYERS
BUT THEY MAKE LOUSY FORESTS.
THANKS!

By putting a "no junk mail" sign on your letter box you can cut junk mail by around 90 per cent.

Why not make a sticker to put on your front door today?

Here are a few ideas.

Don't charge your phone overnight

Sorry. Extra energy doesn't equal extra whizzy super powers (nice as that would be).

Most mobile phones are fully charged in under two hours. But in Britain we waste £47 million a year charging them all night.

Don't. We all need our zzz's. That includes you, Mobie.

Don't start a war

We make 216 choices every day. Try and make the right ones.

Don't ~~*~~ worry if you make a mistake

(sometimes these things have a way of working out...)

It was 1886 and pharmacist John Pemberton just couldn't get his magical medicine to work. It was supposed to cure tiredness and sore teeth but about the only thing going for it was that it tasted good. **It was Coca-Cola. Which now sells a billion drinks a day.**

When little Frank Epperson was asked to stir a fruit drink by his mum in 1905, he thought better of it and went off to play. It stood overnight on the porch.

By morning it had frozen stiff with the spoon stuck straight up. Frank was in trouble. **And the world had the popsicle.**

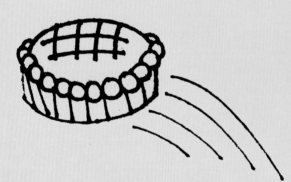

Some college students in America so loved the Frisbie Pies from the famous Frisbie Bakery that they would not only eat them, but play with the tins afterwards. Their favourite game was throwing pie dishes to each other yelling "Frisbie" to warn others. **It caught on.**

In 1928, Scottish scientist Alexander Fleming left an experiment by an open window. By morning his bacteria samples had gone mouldy. But instead of throwing them out, he looked closer and found that the mould was gradually dissolving the harmful bacteria. **Turns out he'd only gone and discovered penicillin – the wonder antibiotic used to save billions of lives.**

In 1853 New York there was a very picky customer. And a very grumpy chef. The customer demanded that his potatoes be cut thinner and fried longer. Furious, the chef cut them very thin, fried them for ages and covered them in salt. The customer asked for more. **Hooray! The crisp was born.**

Christopher Columbus was an explorer looking for Asia. But in 1492 he sailed the wrong way and ended up in an entirely different continent. Happily for him, he didn't realise at the time and announced, quite smugly, that, ho hum, here he was in Asia. **And so it was that America was discovered.**

Walking across deserts is thirsty work. So, hundreds of years ago, an Arabian merchant had an idea. He'd carry his precious milk in a pouch made from a sheep's stomach. But chemicals from the pouch and the heat of the desert turned the milk into cheese. **Lovely on toast. Crummy if you want a drink.**

Walking on a ship deck in 1943 an engineer watched, interested, as a coiled spring fell to the floor and sort of slinked around. Hmm. He thought. **Later he and his wife made their own spiral at home, dropped it from the top step and watched it slinky-dink down to the bottom step. Of almost every house in America.**

Action #125

Talk rubbish to your parents

Next time your parents say, "Haven't you cleaned your room?", say, "I'm glad you brought that up. I've been meaning to talk to you about cleaning up your habits!"

Glass bottles are totally recyclable. But in landfill they will never decompose

TIP: you can find out more at www.recyclenow.com

60% amount of recyclable rubbish in our bins

Illustration: Matthew Hodson

61

Write a letter

Reasons why a letter can be better:

You can't put a text message on the wall.

You can't re-read a phone conversation.

Who ever heard of a love-email?

PS

Of course you could call. Or send a text.

But everyone loves a letter.

Dear Friend / **Enemy** / Politician / **Mum**

I thought that I should write to you
to say that: you owe me money / I'd
like to be friends / I will not stand
for global warming / **I owe you money**.

The situation is less than ideal and
from now on I will be: chasing you /
not chasing you / writing to you
every day / **begging your forgiveness**.

I hope you understand that I am:
skint / **keen to make a new start** /
a future taxpayer/ **your only child**.

Lots of love

Me

Recycle your toys

There are millions of forgotten toys
in bedrooms all over the world.
Unused. Unloved. Under the bed.
It doesn't have to be this way. Give
them away. Swap them.

Love your toys. And when you're
done lovin', set them free.

There's life in
the old bear yet!

𝍷𝍷𝍷𝍷 𝍷𝍷𝍷𝍷 𝍷𝍷𝍷𝍷
𝍷𝍷𝍷𝍷 𝍷𝍷𝍷𝍷 𝍷𝍷𝍷𝍷
𝍷𝍷𝍷𝍷 𝍷𝍷𝍷𝍷 𝍷𝍷𝍷𝍷
𝍷𝍷𝍷𝍷 𝍷𝍷𝍷𝍷 |||

Involve everyone

Some things work better when you do them with lots and lots of people – Mexican waves, football matches, changing the world.

This action is one of those things.

> Create a story full of interesting twists and turns by adding just three words and then passing it on to someone else.
> The more people you get involved, the better the story gets.
>
> Here's one to get you in the mood.
>
> (The only tricky bit is making sure your story ends at the same place as the page!)

ONCE THERE WAS...

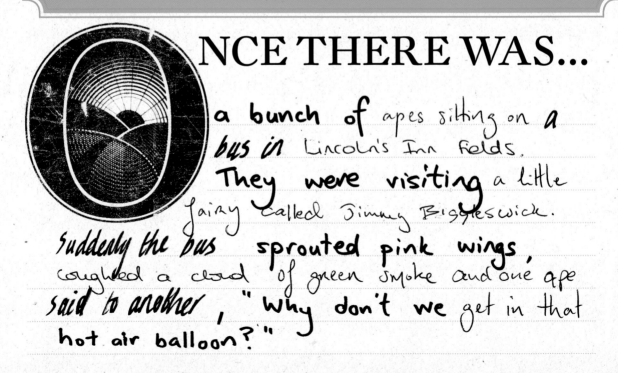

a bunch of apes sitting on a bus in Lincoln's Inn Fields. They were visiting a little fairy called Jimmy Bigglesvick. Suddenly the bus sprouted pink wings, coughed a cloud of green smoke and one ape said to another, "Why don't we get in that hot air balloon?"

As they floated an enormous winged **sellotape dispenser appeared.**

"Oh No! Jimmy is Stuck to the double-sided scotch." Lets rescue him".

Annabel the Ape has an irrational **phobia of giant** adhesives which fly.

So she decided to blindfold herself take a knitting needle and pop their blue spotty balloon **and red trombone**, trying to escape.

Down they fell. The apes screamed "What are you DOING? Silly old Annabel! And stupid phobia!! **where's my broccoli?"**

Jimmy jumps off. The tape unravels. He manages to **grab a cloud** and swing onto **the falling balloon.**

"where's my glasses?" shouted Angus Ape "**They have disappeared!**"

"He only thinks **about his hair. That pesky ape!**"

Meanwhile, Mrs Bigglesuick catches the balloon, **uses the sellotape,** says *Abracadabra* **and patches it up.** All the apes and the Bigglesuicks start to breakdance. Annabel and Angus **fall in love** and all lived happily **ever after.** Broccoli and all!

Speak football

Yes, you're right. Football is a game and not a language. Silly us.

But kicking a ball around is a great way of talking to people who might not understand you.

There are 6,000 languages in the world. Football speaks every one of them.

CIAO

SA

ADAAB

HELLO

HOLA

WUNMAN NJINDE

Illustration: Marcus Walters

in and around

Knit with someone

Two needles are needed to knit.
And that's what you get in the kit,
And also, it's true,
When knitters are two,
There's chatter and tales as you sit.

Illustration: Tori Flower

...and through and OFF...

Add your own action

Oh thank goodness you're here. We've been waiting for you. Holding your page. You see we're one author short of a book. One action short too. And it's the most important, because it's yours.

So. What's the one thing you would ask one million people to do to change the world? Take your time (writers always do). Then go tell all your friends you've just finished writing your first book.

I'd like one million people to...

Added your action?
Don't keep it to yourself.
Log onto www.wearewhatwedo.org
and tell the world.

Action #101
Make someone smile

Action #102
Walk your dad

Action #103
Grow something & eat it

Action #104
Stand up for something

Action #109
Layer up

Action #110
Cook a meal from scratch

Action #111
Love your stuff

Action #112
Go to more parties

Action #117
Read with a pal

Action #118
Don't sing in the shower

Action #119
Play

Action #120
Give lots of compliments

Action #125
Talk rubbish to your parents

Action #126
Write a letter

TO:
My friend / Enemy / Mum / Politician / Dog / Me

Action #127
Recycle your toys

Action #128
Involve everyone

Action #105
Switch things off when you leave the room

Action #106
Test your teacher

Action #107
Look closer

Action #108
Be friendly in sign language

Action #113
Ask "Why?"

Action #114
Love where you live

Action #115
Teach your granny to text

Action #116
Find out about your food

Ghana!

Kent!

Action #121
Stop junk mail

I ♥ TREES

no junk mail please

Action #122
Don't charge your phone overnight

Help us. We need our sleep too.

Action #123
Don't start a war

Action #124
Don't worry if you make a mistake

Don't worry

Action #129
Speak football

ADAAB NÎ HÂO

HOLA CZESC

Action #130
Knit with someone

Action #131
Add your own action

I'd like one million people to...

Let us know how many of these you've done at

www.wearewhatwedo.org

About We Are What We Do

We Are What You Do believes that it is not just politicians, institutions and big business that change the world – it is also ordinary people like you and me.

We are creating a global movement of doing and changing; doing small actions and changing big problems.

Back in 2003, we asked a simple question: "What would you ask one million people to do to change the world?" Thousands of people responded and the result was our bestselling book, *Change the World for a Fiver – 50 actions to change the world and make you feel good*, now sold all over the world.

You might have also seen the "I'm NOT a plastic bag" shopping bags we created with Anya Hindmarch to bring to life the first action in the book, "decline plastic bags".

Find out more about all our other projects at

www.wearewhatwedo.org

Who are we?
We are what we do.

THANK YOUS

Lots of people helped us with this book and to each and every one of you – THANK YOU! In particular, we would like to give a huge thank you to:

The Department for Children, Schools and Families (DCSF) for their support on our original edition, *Teach Your Granny to Text & Other Ways to Change the World*.

The Times for their ideas, energy and enthusiasm.

Special thanks to thousands of teachers, schools, youth workers and young people that have worked with us on this book. Over 1,000 schools were involved in creating this book and the final thirty actions were thought up by children and young people at…

Gilwern Primary School, Gwent; Whitehead Primary School, County Antrim; Ellacombe School, Devon; Dereham Neatherd High School, Norfolk; All Hallows RC Business and Enterprise College, Lancashire; Godwin Junior School, London; St Andrew's CE Primary School, East Sussex; Ringwood School, Hampshire; St Matthew's Academy, London; City and Islington Sixth Form College, London; St Theresa's Catholic Primary School, Sheffield; Westgate School, Lancashire; Calverton Primary School; Community Links Southern Road After School Club, London; St Andrew's CE Primary School; St Mary's First School, West Sussex; The Billericay School, Essex; St Thomas' Clapham, London; St Mary's First School, West Sussex; St Angela's Ursuline School, London; Merchant Taylors Junior School, Stanfield; New Vic Newham Sixth Form College, London Roxeth First and Middle School, Middlesex; Essex Road Primary School, London; St John the Baptist School, London; St Winefride's Primary School, London; Ashlawn Sixth Form, Rugby; Gateway Primary School, London; St Theresa's Catholic Primary School, South Yorkshire; St Joseph's RC Primary School, South Yorkshire; St Mark's Catholic Primary School, Suffolk; St Bonaventures, London; Hessle High School, East Yorkshire; Cwmtawe Comprehensive, Pontardawe; Tottenhall Infant School, London; Christchurch Primary School, Essex; Tollgate Primary School, London and Sudell Primary School, Darwen.

We also have some very special help from…

Helen Matthews, Lois Stokes, John Smith, the D'Rozzaro-Grays, Scilla Morgan, Jenny Beeching, Jenny Wilks, Fidelma Boyd , Paul Jackson, Dave Smithers, Tom Canning, Zuhayb Ahmed, Steve Wilks, Peg Probert, Ishlal Lawrence, Jane Ray and Kate Phillips.

We are also very grateful to The Aldridge Foundation and *v* which have supported We Are What We Do's education and youth programmes.

We Are What We Do team - Eugenie Harvey, Nick Stanhope, David Robinson, Nicole van den Eijnde, Tori Flower, Mike Daley, Ella Wiggans and Frances Clarke.

We Are What We Do board of directors – Giles Gibbons, David Robinson, Stanley Harris, Eugenie Harvey and Nick Stanhope.

WHAT NEXT?

If you're here it's because you've either
a) got lost
b) got bored
c) are Japanese and start books from the back
or
d) have come to the end.

Of course it's not really the end.

It's just the beginning.

This is the bit where you visit us online at

www.wearewhatwedo.org

Where you can...

◎ Meet We Are What We Do and say "hello!"

◎ **Put together your very own action tracker**

◎ Share all your world-changing activities with the world

◎ **Launch your own We Are What We Do creative campaign**

◎ Get hold of amazing stuff to do in lessons and give to your teacher (assuming that they have passed their "Action 106" to your satisfaction!!!)

◎ **Tell your "Action 128" to the world**

◎ Send us your ideas for "Action 131"

◎ **Put your "Action 114" on the map**

◎ Find out where we got all our facts, figures and stats from